Weather to Remember

CONTENTS

NATIONAL GEOGRAPHIC
School Publishing
Hampton-Brown

Words with -**y**

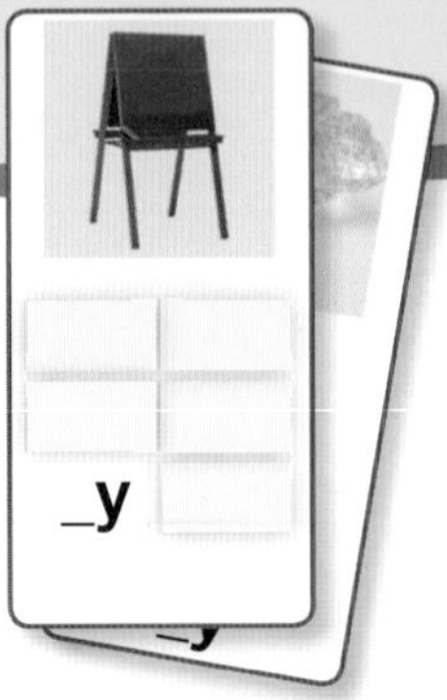

Look at each picture. Read the words.

Example:

cr**y**

happ**y**

dr**y**

lad**y**

sk**y**

wind**y**

High Frequency Words
also
blue
every
fall
family
first
many
most
mountain
only

Key Words

Look at the picture. Read the sentences.

Snowy Day Fun

1. My **family** lived on a **mountain**.
2. **Every** snowy day was fun!
3. One cold day, the sky was **blue**.
4. In **only** a little while, the **first** flakes began to **fall**.
5. We got our **many** sleds and rode them **most** of the day.
6. We **also** made a snowman!

What fun things would your family do on a snowy day?

Phonics Games
NGReach.com

A Big Blizzard

by Malik Patel

Snow may fall many times in winter. Most snow is pretty and fun to play in.

But snowy days can also be risky. When a winter storm gets quite bad, we call it a blizzard. Not every blizzard is really bad. But some are quite nasty!

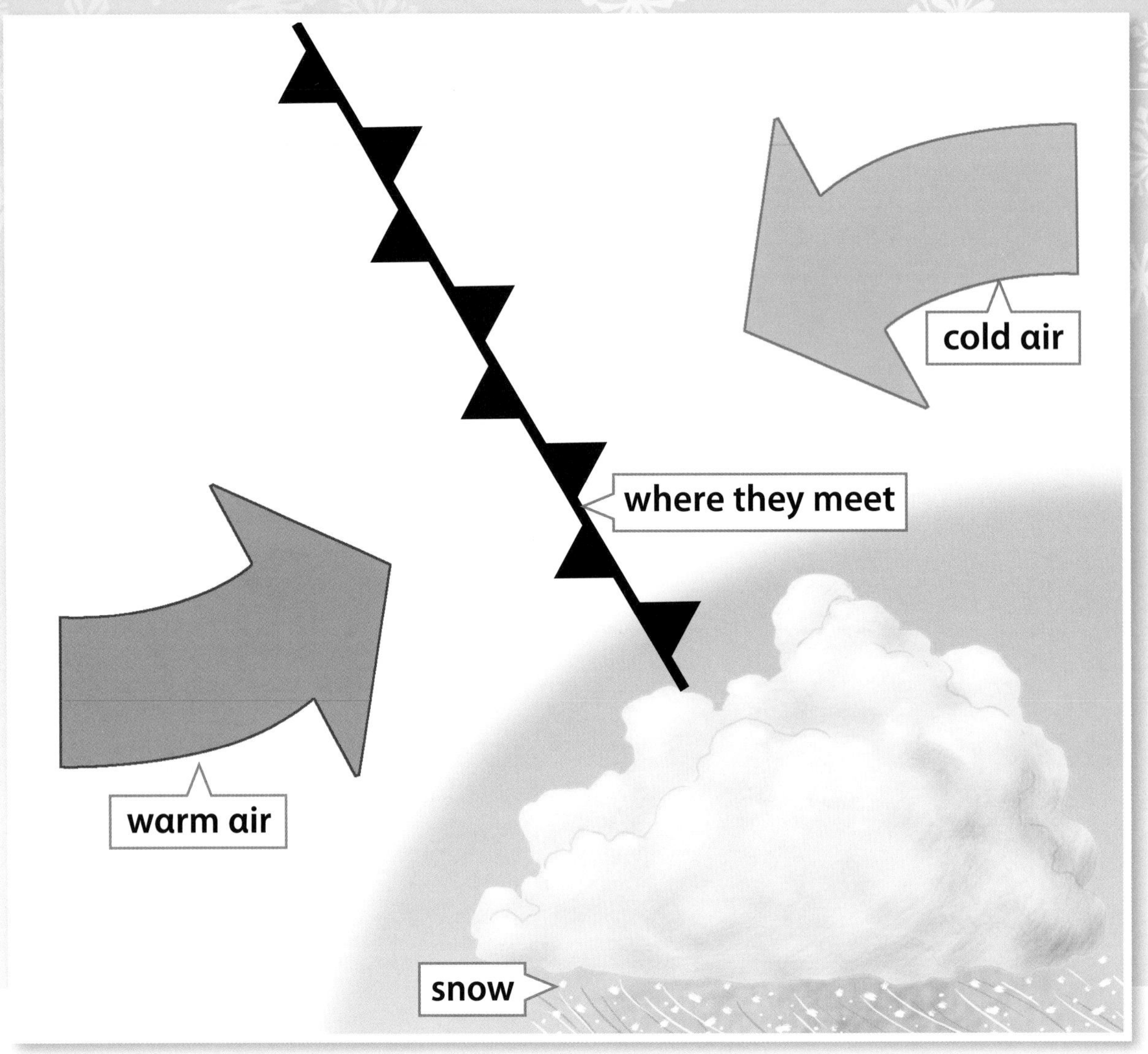

What makes a storm a blizzard? Most blizzards start when freezing air slams into warm air. Cold, windy air quickly fills the skies. If the air is really cold and wet, snow will fall.

Wind, not snow, makes a blizzard. Why is that? Blizzards have gusty winds that blow at least 35 miles an hour. As snow falls, it blows round and round. You can only see 1/4 mile at most.

In the winter of 1978, the city of Boston was hit by a really nasty blizzard. The snow fell softly at first. But it did not stop for three days! The cold winds got nasty.

Mighty gusts of the blizzard pushed snow into mountains. The snow hid mailboxes and even buses!

Winds gusted up to 83 miles an hour. People had to stop driving. They were stranded on the roads by the snow. Those still at home gladly stayed there.

On day three, the storm eased. Boston streets were empty. People who were trapped got helped to safety. Some were helped by big tanks!

Homes on the coast got hit badly.

Families still tell about the Blizzard of ’78. Some sad things happened. People lost their homes. Some lost their lives.

But people had fun, too! After the storm, the sky was blue. The air was clean. The snow was, too!

People wanted to help each other. It felt good! For three days, the people of Boston were like a big, happy family. Then the snow melted. But no one ever forgot the "Blizzard of '78"!

Words with -y

Read these words.

baby	day	lady	sky	windy
cry	happy	snowy	street	try

Find the words with **-y**.
Use letters to build them.

t r y

Talk Together

Choose words from the box above to tell your partner about what you see in the picture.

I see a windy day.

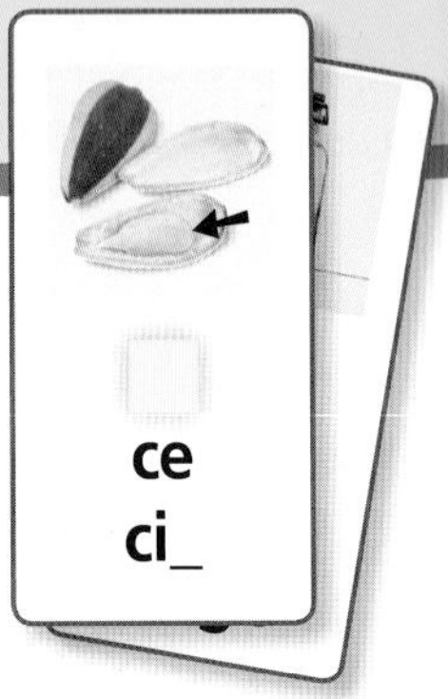

Words with Soft c and g

Look at each picture. Read the words.

Example:

cement

city

gym

bri**dge**

i**ce**

ju**dge**

Practice High Frequency Words

High Frequency Words
also
blue
every
fall
family
first
many
most
mountain
only

Key Words

Read each paragraph. Match them to the pictures.

Road Trip

My **family** takes a road trip **every** year. One trip was to the **mountains** in the **fall**. It was the **first** time I had seen leaves change. They are so pretty next to the **blue** sky!

We **also** took a trip to the beach. We spent **most** of the time swimming. We saw **many** shells but **only** one sand crab!

Which would you like most—the beach or the mountains?

Phonics Games

NGReach.com

The Blue Ridge Parkway

by Dee Wallis

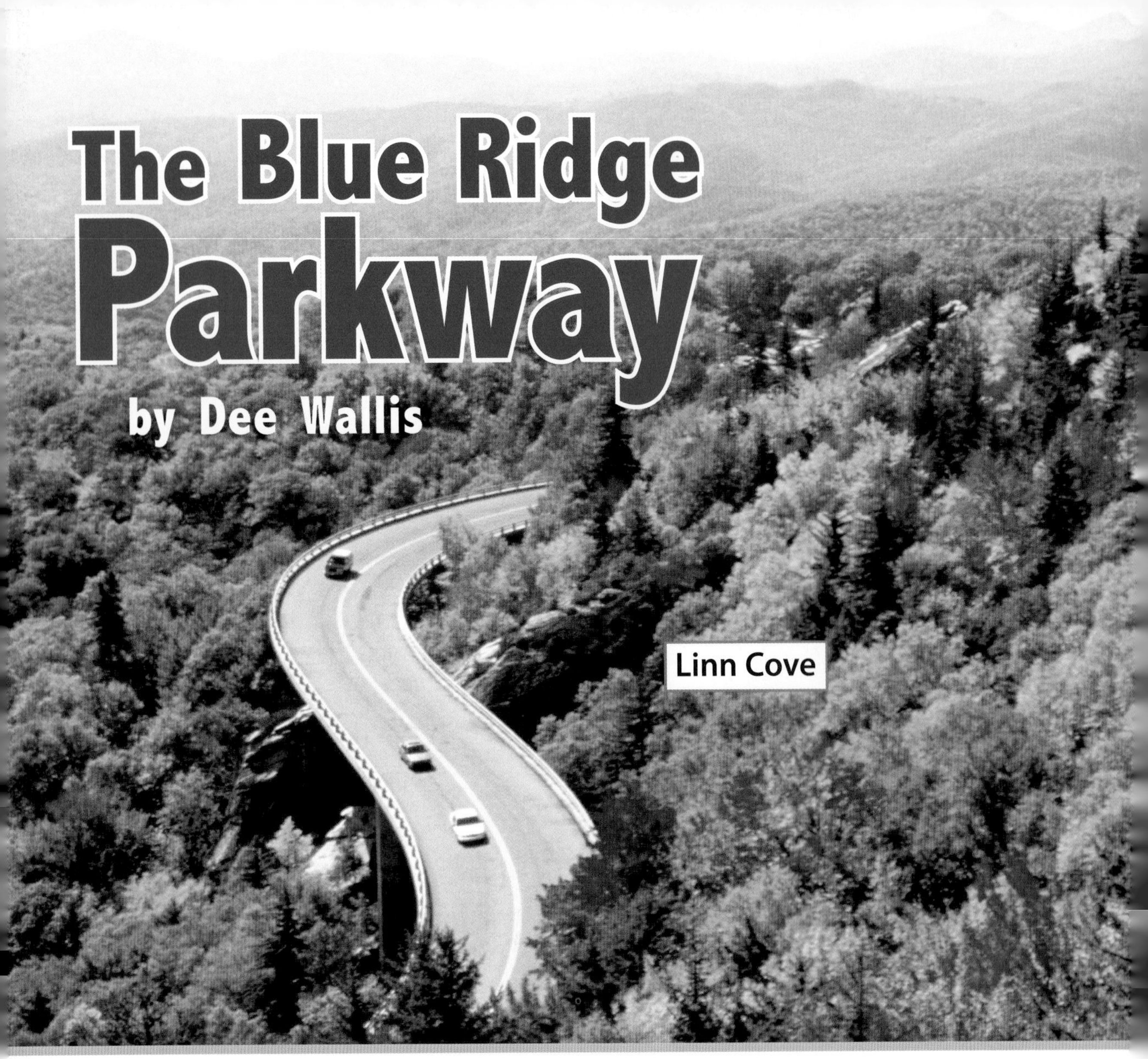

The Blue Ridge Parkway is a great place to visit. This twisting 469-mile road is filled with pretty sights. And it changes with every season!

Let's begin our trip where the road was finished. It's the nice 7-1/2-mile stretch at Linn Cove.

The bridge at Linn Cove is high up, at 4,100 feet. It crosses an old, rocky mountain. People did not want to change the mountain face to fit in the bridge, so it is S-shaped. Lots of concrete and piles of cash went into making this bridge!

In fall, the bright leaves are really nice at Linn Cove. They edge the side of the road.

In winter, snow and ice keep most people off the parkway. Miles of road may be closed on the mountains. Then it is a place filled with peace.

Then spring comes! The first sunny days bring people back to the parkway. They can't wait to get on the road and leave the city behind.

Our spring stop is Mabry Mill. Here, we can see what life was like in 1903. Spring flowers make this pretty site very, very nice!

After we visit Mabry Mill, we can spend the night at Rocky Knob. We will not find a fancy lodge there. We can only stay in a log cabin!

Summer is not too hot on the Blue Ridge Parkway. Many people go to Craggy Gardens to hike and also to see the bright flowers.

We will look for a sunny ledge at Craggy Gardens. With a good seat, a picnic lunch, and so much to see, we will not budge all day!

The Blue Ridge Parkway changes with the seasons. It is a fine place to visit at all times of the year. Maybe some day your family will decide to take a trip on this road. ❖

Words with Soft c and g

Read these words.

bridge	dancing	fudge	ice	tea
cream	fancy	gems	quilts	

Find the words with the soft **c** and soft **g** sounds. Use letters to build them.

b r i d g e

Talk Together

People on the Blue Ridge like to celebrate! Choose words from the box above to tell your partner what you would do at Fall Fun Time.

I would like to see the fancy quilts.
I would like to get some ice tea.

Family Trip

Every time your family takes a trip, you go to different places. If you are going to a place for the first time, you need directions. With a partner, practice giving and following directions.

1. Player 1 chooses a place on the map. He or she asks for directions.
2. Player 2 gives directions from the star ☆ to the place.
3. If the directions work, Player 2 gets a point.
4. Then Player 2 asks for directions to a place. Player 1 gives directions.
5. Go to all the places. At the end, the player with the most points wins.

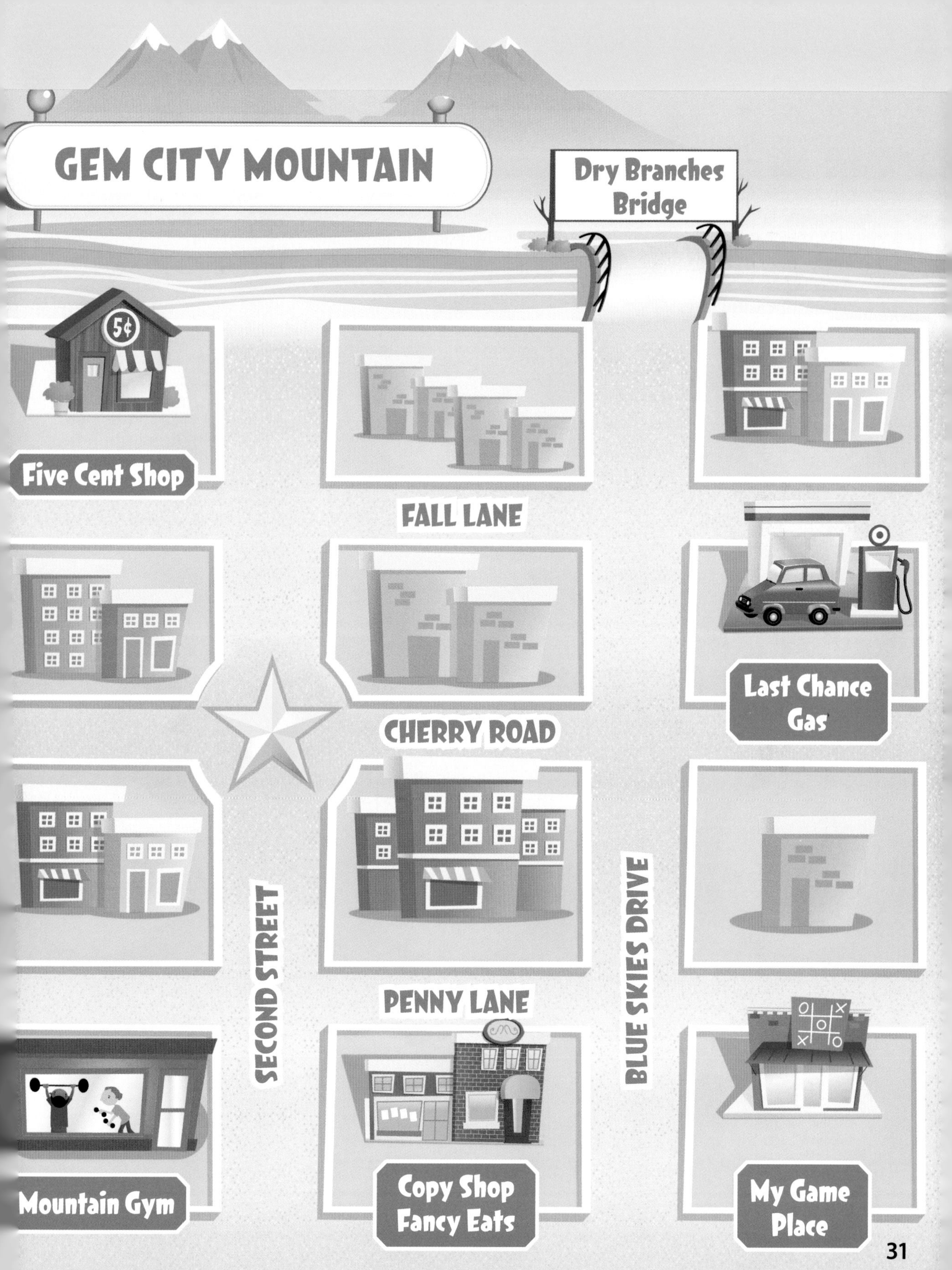
GEM CITY MOUNTAIN
Dry Branches Bridge
5¢
Five Cent Shop
FALL LANE
Last Chance Gas
CHERRY ROAD
SECOND STREET
BLUE SKIES DRIVE
PENNY LANE
Mountain Gym
Copy Shop
Fancy Eats
My Game Place

Acknowledgments
Grateful acknowledgment is given to the authors, artists, photographers, museums, publishers, and agents for permission to reprint copyrighted material. Every effort has been made to secure the appropriate permission. If any omissions have been made or if corrections are required, please contact the Publisher.

Photographic Credits
CVR Mircea Bezergheanu/Shutterstock. **2** (bcr) Jose Luis Pelaez Inc/Blend Images/Alamy Images. (bl) DAJ/Getty Images. (br) jstudio/iStockphoto. (cl) George Doyle/Getty Images. (tcr) Ian Shaw/Alamy Images. (tl) PhotoDisc/Getty Images. **3** Liz Garza Williams/Hampton-Brown/National Geographic School Publishing. **4** Image Source. **5** Digital Vision/Getty Images. **7** Tim Laman/National Geographic Image Collection. **8** Boston Globe/John Blanding/Landov. **9** Boston Globe/Landov. **10** AP Images. **11** AP Images. **12** Boston Globe/Bill Brett/Landov. **13** Boston Globe/Landov. **14** Boston Globe/Stan Grossfeld/Landov. **15** Liz Garza Williams/Hampton-Brown/National Geographic School Publishing. **16** (bcr) DigitalStock/Corbis. (bl) Corbis. (br) Image Source Black/Jupiterimages. (cl) Stephan Zabel/iStockphoto. (tcr) John Foxx Images/Imagestate. (tl) Keith Webber Jr./iStockphoto. **17** (b) Liz Garza Williams/Hampton-Brown/National Geographic School Publishing. (l) DigitalStock/Corbis. (r) Guillen Photography/Travel/USA/Florida/Alamy Images. **18-19** Andre Jenny/Alamy Images. **20** Robert Glusic/age fotostock. **21** DigitalStock/Corbis. **22** Visions of America, LLC/Alamy Images. **23** Andre Jenny/Alamy Images. **24** (bg) SuperStock. (inset) Brian Vanderpool/Alamy Images. **25** Jeff Greenberg/Alamy Images. **26** Rob & Ann Simpson/Visuals Unlimited. **27** Pat & Chuck Blackley/Alamy Images. **28** (bl) Andre Jenny/Alamy Images. (br) Rob & Ann Simpson/Visuals Unlimited. (tl) DigitalStock/Corbis. (tr) Visions of America, LLC/Alamy Images. **29** (t) Liz Garza Williams/Hampton-Brown/National Geographic School Publishing.

Illustrator Credits
6, Dartmouth Publishings; **3**, **15**, **29** Jan Bryan Hunt; **8**, **19**, **25**, **27** Mapping Specialists Ltd; **30-31** Don Tate

National Geographic School Publishing
Hampton-Brown
www.NGSP.com

Printed in the USA.
Quad Graphics, Leominster, MA

ISBN: 978-0-7362-8073-0

17 18 19
10 9 8 7 6